DEC 3rd/2010

To Katherine

I hope you find my Business Parable relevant in some way.

Best Wishes

Bill Mcliah

Not Another

Business Book!

From Selling to Helping...
A Success Story Paradigm

William Meloche

Outer Banks Publishing Group
Outer Banks ● Raleigh

Published in the United States by

Outer Banks Publishing Group

Outer Banks • Raleigh

www.outerbankspublishing.com

Email: william@williammeloche.com

Website: http://www.williammeloche.com

416 922-2692

This book is a work of fiction. Although the names of a few people are real, most of the names and events are a product of the author's imagination. Any resemblance to actual persons, living or dead is not necessarily coincidental.

This book may be purchased online at

www.amazon.com

SECOND EDITION

ISBN: 978-0-9829931-9-4

Book Design

Soulutions Inc.

Toronto, Ontario, Canada

416 340-1000

To my wife, Ann,
whose love, encouragement,
and patience have made
this book possible.

TABLE OF CONTENTS

PROLOGUE – A SIMPLE BIG IDEA

"Most businesses are no more than one big deal away from being on more solid ground"

- My accountant Bernie

W e are living and competing in a complex world. We've seen increasingly uncertain times characterized as "the new normal" – an era of constant change. Economic transitions and instant communication have accelerated the pace of that change while massive information overload adds to the clutter.

This is bound to have an impact on the relationship between suppliers and our business-to-business customers. This book will suggest that the answer to that dilemma is to go to targeted customers with a "big idea" that extends beyond providing our product or service. In effect, we should offer to help them serve their customer - usually an end user.

Let's call it a common pursuit.

Our storyline will show how that approach can

become a crucial differentiator in this world where breakthrough products are on their way to becoming commodities before they're ready to launch.

Bouncing around from one crisis to another makes the improvement of B2B relationships a formidable challenge.

We have been trying to adapt. We've learned to create strategic alliances, share best practices, and rationalize the daylights out of more integrated business strategies. And when the details threaten to get beyond us, we call in consultants, trading impressive fees for equally impressive, sometimes inscrutable, reports. I know because, although I've sat on both sides of the table, I am one of those consultants.

RELATIONSHIP INNOVATION

So here's a secret. After embracing change, like any right-thinking professional - and advising clients to do the same - I sometimes wonder: How are we consultants helping suppliers forge more productive B2B relationships? It's tempting to believe that as the challenges get more complicated, so should the solutions. I believe that our times call for a seemingly obvious approach - present a success story based on helping them help their customer - and bring it to life.

That is my definition of <u>Relationship Innovation</u>.

Coming up with that "big strategic idea" is the challenging part - so that's where I help my clients the most. I know from personal experience that pulling it off can dramatically change the fortunes of anyone who provides a product or a service to a B2B customer.

I have written this book to impart a real-world process for creating, closing and implementing business-to-business relationships that can put any enterprise on more solid ground.

I know something about that from founding, building, and selling a global communications company and from helping other businesses create and close groundbreaking B2B deals. There was a time when having a good product could assure business success. Then we moved on to an era where our products needed to become solutions, so problem solving became the order of the day. Generating breakthrough sales results in the new normal will be more about helping our B2B customers get where they want to go at a strategic level. Products and solutions will continue to be important, but "relationship innovation" at a strategic level will be even more important.

A groundbreaking relationship is defined from a supplier's perspective as a business deal that generates incremental revenue beyond any existing account relationship by a factor of ten - or another way of putting it - "the biggest deal we've ever made."

What's going on in the economy can have a profound effect on making such deals. But whether in good times or bad, let's admit that hitting one out of the park is getting harder, and when it happens, the victory can be less predictable and more short-lived than we'd like. I also believe that when companies miss their goals, the reasons can often be traced to a management team that's looking in the wrong direction. In a culture geared toward elaborate solutions, it's easy to forget that the best answers might still be found in keeping things simple.

A COMMON PURSUIT

T he story you are about to read suggests that we dust off a seldom used tool in our calamitous world - our collective imagination. You may have trouble relating to that notion because like most entrepreneurs, you may be more obsessed with your technology, your product or your service than coming up with a big strategic idea for someone else.

So let's make it easier by introducing you to Jeremy Swift, a central figure in this story who is a CEO with an MBA and a PhD in medical robotics. We met at a time when he was in danger of seeing his business go under. It wasn't a good moment for either of us. Jeremy is something of an acquired taste - driven, impatient and downright rude. God knows what he thinks of me; we're still working it out. Even so, he can be a pretty creative guy - when he gives himself time - and I owe him a lot because the events following our meeting led to this story.

A few words about the protagonist in this story - me. Meloche Communications began in the early eighties as a corporate media production house. I sold the business 18 years later after morphing it into a multi-million-dollar communications agency (with offices in Toronto, New York, Chicago, and London, England), and along with my wife and our yellow Lab, retired to the gated, private country-club life of Rancho Mirage, California and Lake Tahoe, Nevada. It was the fulfillment of a dream and in many ways idyllic. It was also a mistake. These are communities where former leaders of commerce go to improve their golf handicaps and fade away. On any given day, the club flag rides at half-mast and the most meaningful discussion revolves around, "who moved that ball washer on number six?"

After a dozen years living what many would think of as the good life, I was eager to get back to the real world. Except the new millennium had arrived with a digital bang, and learning to communicate in this computer-dominated environment turned out to be an unexpected struggle. Nobody had enough time. Face-to-face meetings had become less common and far too rushed. I found myself moaning about the disappearance of thoughtful, back-and-forth exchanges that could stimulate innovative solutions. While I imagined returning like Moses from the desert, I was in danger of being seen as another seasoned curmudgeon, very much out of step.

Early in my reentry, an investment banker suggested getting together with Jeremy Swift since he had a promising young company in trouble, and I knew how to grow a business from scratch. It was a classic worlds-colliding scenario. Yet for all the pain, we're both better for it, and I believe it has produced something helpful to anyone who wants to improve business performance. The lessons apply most immediately to small and mid-sized firms, agile enough to stop and think. But there's also something for the senior management of large, publicly traded companies, eager to rediscover their entrepreneurial roots by adopting a more innovative approach to their B2B relationships.

One caution: this story isn't meant to be taken literally. Some names have been held back or changed for good reason, and none of the events mentioned here unfolded exactly as described. That includes anything to do with Jeremy Swift. Readers will also come across a character named Oliver B. Adams - aka Obvious Adams - who first came to life in 1916 on the fiction pages of the *Saturday Evening Post*. Mr. Adams is also central to the story, and even though he doesn't exist in a flesh-and-blood sense, I believe I know him and hope he'll continue to be part of my life. So what follows might seem like a fantasy, but it's a distillation of the business relationships I've been exposed to throughout my career. While it all happened, it's not *real*. I can only promise that it's true.

Act One

Our protagonist makes new friends

and

bites off more than he can chew

THE RUDE AWAKENING

T he meeting was set for 7 a.m. - breakfast at the Adams Roadhouse in North Carolina's Research Triangle. At the time, I worked out of both Raleigh, North Carolina and Toronto, Ontario in the rather specialized consulting field of "relationship innovation." I may be the only consultant on the planet with that specialty. Jeremy Swift had agreed to give me exactly one hour, and he was late.

To kill time, I chatted with the owner, a gentleman of uncertain age, trading small talk about life in the Triangle. He had a slightly formal, matter-of-fact manner that made people feel instantly at home. As he poured me a second cup of coffee, I was reminded about the CEO of a financial services conglomerate who took my advice and positioned his company as providing "the security of a big bank with the personal touch of a general store." This diner had that solid, welcoming feel, which evaporated with the arrival of my new client.

Jeremy Swift dropped his briefcase beside the table, waved off the owner, and continued talking into his smart phone.

"Their machine's not anywhere near as good as ours. The chief of surgery should know that. I'm not losing another goddamn sale to those guys. Fix this."

He slammed the phone on the table. It immediately started buzzing.

"Yeah, talk," he said, returning it to his ear. While listening he looked at me and asked, "So what do you think of the new MX-series robot?"

In fairness to Jeremy, I wasn't in a great mood. I was still wrestling with the return to active duty and this had been a week full of impatient clients looking for "methodologies" and "deliverables" without much interest in the underlying problems. Here was another one, ready to jump into the "metrics", a phone strapped to his head and 30 minutes late.

Deciding to be equally blunt, I said, "I'd rather spend the time we have left talking about the customer you just lost."

"That means you have reservations about the technology?"

"It means we don't need to go into the technology

11

right now," I replied.

"Yeah, I'll look over the stats and get back," said Jeremy, flipping the phone lid shut and getting up.

"I've got better things to do than pay for a so-called strategist with no interest in my product." On his way out, he narrowly missed knocking down the owner.

Laying a menu in front of me, the owner said, "Not such a good morning for you?"

"Obviously."

"It's funny you should say that," he replied, "Obvious, yes."

He tucked an order pad into his apron and asked, "Have you ever heard of Obvious Adams?"

"Not that I recall."

"Well, Obvious Adams had been a business consultant, famous in his day for telling people what they already knew. Hence his name. Actually, he was a fictional character in a Saturday Evening Post series but for a while, became something of a business icon."

I nodded politely. The connection escaped me.

"So what were you going to say to that fellow before he rushed off?"

"I was about to suggest that when you're building a business, products can take a back seat to relationships."

"I would not be surprised if he knew that, deep down," said the owner. "Perhaps at your next meeting, you could try persuading him to pay more attention to what he already knows."

"Next meeting?" I figured Jeremy Swift wasn't the only one who'd lost some business that morning.

"Oh, I am certain you will see him again. He left his briefcase.

WHO IS OBVIOUS ADAMS?

Obvious Adams was first published as a short story in the Saturday Evening Post in April, 1916. Though it was the story of an advertising man, it was quickly recognized as presenting a germ idea basic to outstanding success in the business world and the professions.

Harper & Brothers brought out the story in book form in September of 1916 and the book had healthy sales.
In reviewing it, the New York Times said, "The young man who is going to seek his fortune in the advertising business should have Obvious Adams for a handbook. Indeed, any young man who is going to seek his fortune in anything might be aided by the common sense and business acumen displayed in this little volume."

"Obvious Adams" soon became a legendary character. He was quoted in business conferences and at board meetings. Heads of companies wrote the author to ask if the hero of the story was a real person; that if he was they wanted to engage his services. His "obviousness" influenced the thinking of some of the outstanding industrial leaders of the day - men of the caliber of Elbert H. Gary, head of U.S. Steel, who read the book and wrote the author an appreciative letter.

*   *from LeadershipNow.com.*

THE CORPORATE STAND UP ACT

In a past life, I'd often been hired as a guest speaker on the subject of strategic communications. (I once popped up on a conference agenda, sandwiched between Alvin Toffler, the author of Future Shock, and Henry Kissinger, the former secretary of state. Since both gentlemen possess infinitely more gray matter than me, it can be assumed some companies put a premium on comic relief.) I was frequently billed as "infotainment"— somewhere between a corporate stand up act and a provider of useful insight.

One of my more popular talks lamented that big companies would retain a professional ad agency to get consistent messaging across to consumers, while coming up with employee communications that were all over the place. It was easy to bring this contradiction to life in ways that resonated with corporate executives and even made them laugh.

Afterwards I'd get comments like, "Loved the talk, but you didn't say anything we didn't know before." This was

15

often followed by an admission that even though they understood the link between internal and external messaging, they weren't very good at it. And those responses often led to new account relationships. I'd made a good living off the fact that basic ideas, no matter how familiar, could still open doors and make people think.

SIMPLE COMMON SENSE

Driving back from the Adams Roadhouse, I flashed back on this experience. The owner had reminded me that there was something worthwhile in common sense strategies that didn't depend entirely on a mountain of data. I used to have clients who'd spend days making sure a presentation included everything they wanted to say, then watch as their audience sat quiet and glassy-eyed, the details sailing over everybody's head. I'd tell them that no matter how important the content, it was less important than what people were prepared to hear.

Of course they knew that - who didn't? But until I said it, they acted like it applied to somebody else.

Maybe I should be positioning myself as a modern Obvious Adams.

For example, when confronted by a retailer who had trouble attracting customers, Adams was the kind of consultant who would simply suggest that they put up a more visible sign. Why did my bank go under? Ole Obvious might say you shouldn't lend money to people who couldn't pay it back.

I could offer that kind of advice. For me, being obvious was instinctive.

THE TWILIGHT ZONE

T he following week I had another meeting in the Research Triangle and decided to swing by the Adams Roadhouse and thank the owner for steering me in a new direction. But, the Adams Roadhouse wasn't there.

I was sure I'd returned to the right spot, but the building had vanished. I got out my cell and contacted Information. There was no listing. I found a phone book, looked through the white and yellow pages. Nothing. Maybe the Research Triangle was like the Bermuda Triangle and had swallowed up the restaurant, patrons, coffee cups, and all. Or was this my first senior moment? Was it possible I'd imagined it?

I called the investment banker who had suggested the diner. He remembered referring me to Jeremy Swift; he didn't recall mentioning a location, and he'd never heard of the Adams Roadhouse. Throughout the rest of the day's meetings, my attention wandered. Some of my clients might have lost their entrepreneurial spirit. I was losing my mind.

That afternoon, back in my office, I got a call from Laurie, my assistant. There was a visitor in the lobby without an appointment. His name was Obvious Adams.

Really?

Moments later, the visitor was seated across from my desk. It was the owner of the Adams Roadhouse.

Adams crossed his legs perfectly relaxed, perfectly at home.

"It's nice to see you again, Bill. I hope you don't mind me dropping in without an appointment."

Playing along, I said, "Since we're going with first names, do you have one or should I just call you Obvious?"

"It's Oliver, thank you. But I am a fictional character and most people just use the name from the original story."

"You don't look fictional to me."

"Sometimes characters take on a life of their own. I suggest we not waste time trying to figure out if I am real or not. That would be counter-productive."

"Counter-productive to what?" I asked. "What do you want?"

"Perhaps we can help each other. I've spent almost a hundred years promoting straightforward business ideas. It has not been easy. When the Saturday Evening Post folded, so did I. I need new material. That's where you come in."

"How so?" I asked.

"When you give a speech, do people think they have already heard everything you've said?

"I suppose."

"Do your simplest ideas produce results for your clients? Are you frustrated because they are suspicious of obvious solutions?"

"Yes," I admitted.

He leaned in. "You are the closest thing to me that's come along in decades. We can help each other. That's important because helping is the most obvious strategy there is."

Weird as this was, Adams had struck a chord and a concept had emerged: "The Help Ethic."

SO WHAT IS THE HELP ETHIC?

Back in the Meloche Communications days, our services had included incentive programs and formal award presentations, sometimes high profile, black-tie affairs. One of our clients was an insurance company that sold policies through independent agents. Every year, we'd host an awards night to recognize the best performers. And every year the same guy would take home the top prize, outselling the next five agents combined. He was the only one to earn a seven-figure income consistently, year after year.

Insurance isn't my thing, but I was curious. Most people

go out of their way to avoid policy pushers. Agents need to put themselves out there, and this guy didn't have a personality that would light up anybody's interest. In fact, he was mild-mannered to the point of invisibility. So what made him different from all the other salespeople? After one of these awards evenings, I asked him.

His answer: "I'm not sure."

I must have looked disappointed because he thought for a moment, "It's probably something to do with people sensing I'm not trying to sell them insurance. I'm really trying to help them."

It dawned on me that the guy wasn't just being modest, that whether he realized it or not, he had stumbled on to something important. Communicating a help ethic had built trust and set him apart from the competition.

I decided to try adopting "the help ethic" as a marketing strategy for my own business. We would no longer sell a catalog of services; we would use whatever skills we had to make things easier for clients and ensure they got what they wanted. It was a culture shift from selling to helping that established trust and fostered a better working relationship. Within five years, what started as an experiment made us the world's largest, most successful communications firm of its kind.

Maybe "The Help Ethic" could be turned into a book, I thought. Obvious Adams and I could get together regularly at his diner and work on the material. I was about to suggest it when it occurred that the Adams Roadhouse didn't exist.

As if reading my mind, Adams threw up an arm and said, "It will exist. And so will I. Every Saturday at 7 a.m. See you there, Bill."

With that, he got up and walked to the door. A little wave and he was gone.

Later, on my way out of the office, I asked Laurie if Obvious Adams had left a business card. She eyed me suspiciously, "Who's Obvious Adams?"

STOPPING TO THINK

O kay, so I really was losing my mind. Our dog Bailey had started avoiding me, and my wife Ann kept asking if something was wrong; I seemed distracted. But crazy or not, I was getting a charge out of preparing for the next meeting with Adams. And I was making progress.

Alvin Toffler once predicted today's business leaders are being pressured to cope with ongoing, accelerating change. It's all about running. Managing large companies has come down to mitigating risk while juggling an expanding range of best practices.

There's little room for mistakes, and little time for creating entrepreneurial strategy. Lou Gerstner did just the opposite with IBM in the 1990s, but he was an exception.

Coming from the outside, and despite having no background in technology, he was able to stand back and look at what was happening before setting Big Blue on a new course. These days, managers are often pulled in too many directions to take that first step - to stop and think about what's most important.

It was all coming together. I wrote down this statement: *"Business success is about adopting the Help Ethic."*

I scratched it out and wrote:

"Business success means you have to <u>stop and think</u> before adopting 'the help-ethic'"

Then for a little zing I added:

"then put it to work to make money."

— § —

On Saturday morning I drove to the original location of Adams Roadhouse. There it was, as promised, with Obvious Adams sitting in a booth, alone.

Pleased that he had managed to resurrect the diner, I said, "If we're going to rewrite your story, maybe you can bring back the *Saturday Evening Post* to publish it."

He smiled, "One step at a time, Bill. How have you been doing?"

"I've come up with a strategic statement," I said, "maybe a title - business success means you have to stop and think before adopting the Help Ethic, then put it to work to make money."

"You are a genius," he exclaimed. "What does it mean?"

"How can you ask that? Isn't it obvious?"

"Just because something is obvious to you, doesn't make it so for anybody else." He gazed toward the ceiling. "Your help ethic sounds lofty of purpose and gentle as a cloud. Your clients may think it naive."

"Yeah, but it works."

"We will have to show people what the words mean. I suggest starting with your friend from the other day, that fellow who left in such a hurry."

IT AIN'T EASY BEING OBVIOUS

O bvious is one of those words that shouldn't need a definition. We all know what it means; yet somebody felt a need to spell it out. If you look in Webster's, there it is: "easily perceived or understood." Shakespeare put it more poetically: "so clear, so shining...it will glimmer through a blind man's eye." As in Thomas Jefferson's declaration that certain truths are "self-evident."

This is where we get into trouble. There's a tendency to confuse the obvious with things that are instinctive: "arising from impulse, spontaneous, unthinking," according to another dictionary.

Unthinking? Not a reputation consultants want to encourage. You don't spend hundreds of billable hours generating reports, and then tell clients your recommendations are based on a hunch. Those eureka moments when brilliant ideas materialize from thin air are pretty rare and something of an illusion.

When Lou Gerstner joined IBM, he found himself at

27

the top of a complex organization with appropriately complex problems. The wisdom of the day said the best outcome would be gotten by breaking up the company and selling it, so his decision to take a different tack put him at odds with the majority of business strategists. Pulling it off made him a visionary; some might say a magician.

Was the solution obvious? Eventually, yes. Was it instinctive? Probably not.

I had a chance to observe Gerstner close-up during his American Express years when he ran its card, travelers check, and travel business. His performance in global meetings was impressive as he confronted large groups of management, sales, marketing, operations, and finance people, bridging their diverse interests in language that was clear, concise, candid, and consistent. This was a leader with a grasp of detail, as well as a viewpoint that spanned the entire organization.

He also refused to limit himself to a one-trick management style. In moving to the CEO spot at RJR Nabisco, he retreated from the growth philosophy that had worked so well at Amex and sold off $11 billion in assets during his first year – a clear recognition of the importance of cash flow. By the time he got to IBM, he was thoroughly familiar with the opposing strategies of growth vs. slash-and-burn, and whatever his preference, he was smart enough to bend to the needs of the day.

In IBM's case, expansion was out of the question, but for Gerstner, the solution didn't rest solely on shedding unprofitable operations. America's favorite computer giant was rich in talent; the problem was focus: the need to reposition itself as an organization willing to put its collective brainpower behind improving its customers' performance. To make the point, Gerstner even rode shotgun on sales calls, while continuing to gather information first-hand. So the turnaround, when it happened, might have looked as though it was pulled from a hat, but it was mostly due to his earlier experience as an IBM corporate customer, followed up by a willingness to question all the facts or all the important ones - before drilling down to a seemingly "obvious" answer.

I had to write some notes for Obvious in a small pad I always carried.

Notes for OA

- Helping clients, an obvious goal. It's worked for me. Others might need convincing.

- The conventional wisdom isn't always wisdom.

- Taking time means looking at the whole picture.

- Facts don't solve problems by themselves. Finding obvious answers takes effort.

SO HOW CAN I HELP?

J eremy Swift's office is a tribute to high-tech achievement. Freshly blasted brick walls. Glass shelves, bare except for the occasional athletic trophy: mostly for individual sports like swimming, tennis, and racquetball. A couple industry awards. A photo from a panel discussion with Larry Page, Steve Jobs, and Jeremy staring at the moderator. Another photo of him sitting at the controls of a small plane. Degrees from MIT and Duke University. A framed *New Yorker* cartoon: a panhandler dropping a coin into his own cup mumbling, "Success breeds success." And on the credenza, a bank of monitors with flashing schematics, a video feed to the robot assembly floor, and stock indicators marching across one screen. It was the Nasdaq that held his interest as he pointed me toward an Eames lounge chair.

"Don't know how you got in here," he said. "I pay people good money to keep guys like you out."

"I have skills," I said, offering the briefcase he'd forgotten at the Adams Roadhouse.

"Thing's mostly a prop. Everything I need is on this." He un-holstered his smart phone. "But thanks. I did go looking for that diner, but I couldn't find it. It just disappeared."

A familiar voice said, *"No need to go into this, Bill."*

I stopped breathing. Across the room, sitting on a leather-aluminum couch was Obvious Adams, himself. The smart phone buzzed and Jeremy put it to his ear.

"You shouldn't be surprised, Bill," said Adams. *"Wherever you go, I will be with you. There is much at stake, and I intend to write down everything. I'm here to help you."*

"Can he see you?" I nodded toward Jeremy.

"No, he can only see and hear you."

Jeremy put down the phone and said, "How's that, again?"

"The diner's in a tricky neighborhood. Easy to miss."

"Yeah, well, there's something I need to deal with, so

thanks again." He moved away from his desk.

I'm not sure who pushed the conversation, Adams or I. One of us blurted out my reason for being there.

"Mr. Swift. I didn't come here to return something you lost, although I'm glad to do it. We got off to a bad start the other day and I'm sorry about that. We can both do better. You have problems; they might be serious. I can find you the answers."

He paused on his way to the door. "Okay, mister-lost-and-found, what do you want? Exactly."

"I want to help you."

And that's how it started. I won't claim that Jeremy immediately bought the idea I could help him or his company. His judgment hadn't been entirely wrong during our few moments at the Roadhouse: I knew little about his company, other than what was on the website, and nothing at all about medical robots. But something about the open-faced quality with which I (or Adams) said "I want to help you" got his attention.

Pointing to the monitors, Jeremy began laying out what he was up against. It was quite the tale of woe, partly aimed at proving I couldn't do much about it.

His company, Swift SurBotics Inc. (SSI), had developed a new robot, the best yet for visualizing body parts in 3D and manipulating delicate instruments. It could revolutionize certain surgeries, but after weeks putting together pitches for UCLA, the Cleveland Clinic, and the Meisner Medical Center, all the deals appeared to be heading south.

It was frustrating. Of all the surgical milestones, Jeremy Swift believed two in particular stood out. The first was anesthesiology; hard to believe we were once so primitive as to put people on a table and cut into them while they were still awake. The second breakthrough might very well be medical robotics. In Jeremy Swift's view, one day we'd look back on surgery without these machines and marvel that such a thing had been done.

Despite the enormity of its discoveries, Swift SurBotics needed a break to establish itself in the marketplace. Creating the MX-series had eaten up huge

R&D dollars - so much that the company was running low on cash, which in turn threatened other projects in the pipeline. Predictably, the shareholders were unhappy. That was a problem: the share price hadn't recovered from the usual year-end, tax-loss selling. The FDA had dragged its feet on approval, delaying the product launch, and the new technology had been slow to take off.

Now, with investor confidence falling, SSI had to boost sales or find more financing. And do it in an unfriendly climate. That's why Jeremy had been talking to an investment banker, and why he'd agreed to see me in the first place. The banker had suggested the meeting, and Jeremy was afraid to look unwilling.

"Don't take it personally, Bill. The man is under pressure. Remember you're here to help," Adams reminded me.

The more Jeremy talked, the more wound up he got. Like many small-cap stocks, SSI was vulnerable to getting shorted into oblivion. But with the industry's most advanced technology, the cash-strapped company had also become a candidate for takeover. One way or another, Jeremy might be losing control of the company he founded; there were rumors the board was thinking about inviting him to exit.

"It makes sense," he said, "bring in a caretaker management, fire a few bodies, shelve some R&D and wait till the MX gets established. Not my style. In this business, if you don't keep moving forward, the competition will. So, mister-I-want-to-help-you, what have you got?"

I had nothing. The scenario he'd outlined was at the edge of my experience and maybe a bit beyond. Obvious Adams cautioned, *"You'll want to avoid rushing into this, Bill. You don't have all the facts."*

So I asked Jeremy, how - with so much to think about - he figured out what to deal with, first.

"Mostly, I worry about everything at once."

HOMEWORK

I n the days following, I plunged into the homework I should have done before meeting Jeremy Swift. Surgical robots had been under development since the mid-1980s and had been used to improve a bunch of procedures: brain biopsies, hip replacements, prostate removal, neurosurgery, heart bypasses. One doctor had even used a robot to take out a gall bladder - the trick being that the doctor was in New York at the time, while the patient was in France. Operation Lindbergh it was called in recognition of the trans-Atlantic connection. Fascinating stuff.

The dog was definitely avoiding me. And conversations with my wife often began with a factoid about people's insides.

"I don't want to hear about fallopian tube reconnection," Ann might say and suggested this would be a good time to visit her daughter in Phoenix.

Luckily I could hang out with my invisible friend; the Saturday meetings with Obvious Adams had become daily events. "You are getting swept away by the details," he warned. "That is good, but at some point you will have to step back."

"Not yet," I said.

Swift SurBotics had one main competitor, Dallas Scientific, a smaller company with less sophisticated technology. The Dallas robot couldn't do as much, but it was more compact, less expensive, and easier to learn, making it better suited to teaching hospitals. These were the arguments raised by Meisner's chief of surgery. Cleveland and UCLA had similar concerns and a longer decision-making process. Of course, SSI could approach other customers, and it was, but the company had invested so much time in going after this business that Jeremy was reluctant to walk away. These were prestigious institutions, any one of which could be the icebreaker he was looking for.

Even though a strategy was nowhere in sight, a few things stood out. With institutional customers, advertising wasn't the force it might be in a mass market. As Jeremy put it, "You don't get these machines at Walgreens; we arm our reps with a boatload of facts and put them in doctors' faces." This was evidence-based medicine on a professional committee level.

For sure, SSI didn't need me to develop a new sales pitch; its people knew more about the product than I could hope to. And if management opted for downsizing over Jeremy's objections, the company had an HR department, plus an outside agency that did most recruiting and could help take the sting out of staff cuts. As for the share price, an investor relations firm was fully primed to sell SSI to the street; all it needed was good news to stimulate interest.

On the communications front, standard practices didn't fit.

Adams asked, "Is that what you want? To help Mr. Swift communicate?"

"It's what I do."

"Communicate with whom?" he asked.

That was a good question. Who should Jeremy be

reaching out to? Customers? Investors? His board of directors? Who was the audience? What was the message?

I had never looked at communications only in the context of words, media and formal channels. While those things are important, a communications strategy should also be about getting messages across to stakeholders on an informal basis. Jeremy was obsessed with selling his product more than delivering a message that says, "I want to help you."

Oliver looked me in the eye and said, "Obviously, helping is the right strategy."

"Yes, but we both know that pulling it off isn't easy."

Jeremy's clients will want help. But by now, I'd picked up as much about the robotics business as I could absorb and I was still short on answers.

It was time to look in another direction.

TARGETING A CUSTOMER

It is claimed that the Ford Motor Company invented just-in-time manufacturing in the 1920s. So when Toyota's senior managers went shopping for ideas to rebuild after World War II, they naturally stopped by the Ford plant in Detroit. They left disappointed. By Japanese standards, there was too much waste, leading to parts shortages, assembly-line bottlenecks, and a cycle of work slowdowns, layoffs, and rehiring.

But they did find inspiration from another American source - Piggly Wiggly, the supermarket retailer with a stock refilling system that kicked in much earlier in the supply chain. Today, Toyota still uses pieces of that original inventory model.

*The **Harvard Business Review** once pointed out that Ikea, the home furnishings multi-national, changed the concept of value by redefining traditional business roles. Ikea enjoys billions in annual sales, yet it doesn't manufacture or assemble anything. It doesn't even deliver. By getting people to put together their own* *furniture, it's turned customers into employees willing to pay for the privilege. To sweeten the deal, Ikea throws in perks like coffee shops, restaurants, free strollers, supervised day-care, and playgrounds. If a product is too big for somebody's car, the company provides special roof racks, for which it charges a rental fee. All in all, a contemporary spin on Tom Sawyer's strategy for painting his fence.*

Suppliers get similar treatment. Once manufacturers become part of the Ikea network, they gain an exclusive relationship with access to technical help, leased equipment, and a computer database that can find raw materials and introduce new business partners. In return, Ikea gets a reliable product source, minus the capital outlay for plant construction.

Whatever you call the result - an extended enterprise, a virtual corporation - it's about integrating the supply chain to everybody's benefit. As I used to say to my golf partners in Rancho Mirage, "I can't do it alone."

— § —

Extracted from a strategy paper I once wrote:

Picture this. You've just spent six months cultivating a customer. Listening. Creating solutions. Going to the wall. The execution has been flawless and now, with a new project in the wings, the customer says: "Great job. Why don't you join the bidding and submit another proposal?" In other words, superb performance has earned nothing more than the right to stand in line with your competitors.

Could I relate this to health care?

U.S. News & World Report recently looked at 5,462 hospitals, ranking each in 16 specialties. Only 173 made the list of the nation's best. The leaders included Johns Hopkins, UCLA, the Mayo Clinic, the Cleveland Clinic, and Massachusetts General. The Meisner Medical Center also scored high, offering the broadest range of surgical services, without topping any one category. But despite its outstanding reputation within the professional community, the lack of awareness among the general public had hurt recent fundraising.

Two Meisner surgeons were world renowned for what's called minimally invasive surgery or MIS - performing operations through tiny keyhole incisions - resulting in less trauma, fewer complications, shorter hospital stays, and faster recovery for patients.

I had more notes for Obvious.

- Good ideas can come from anywhere. Don't limit solutions to robots.

- Message should speak to everybody – customers, staff, investors

- SSI promotes better health care, not just machines. Align goals with customers.

- Help the helpers. Primary target = Meisner Medical Center.

Act Two

Our protagonist discovers what he already

Knows and labors to get out the message

A WILD RIDE

T he next meeting with Jeremy Swift lasted about two minutes. I was hardly into his office when he started shutting down the monitors. "Something's come up in Texas," he said. "Have to get to my plane." There was no further explanation, and reluctant to miss an opportunity, I offered to drive him to the airport.

"Naw, let's take my car. We can talk."

A Porsche 911 is not conducive to thoughtful conversation. With the racing suspension thumping over every pavement crease, it was hard to hold my audience's attention while he multi-tasked as usual and continued checking the mirrors for holes in surrounding traffic. The only saving grace was the fact that the roof was up and Jeremy, to my relief, stuck approximately to the speed limit.

"This is interesting," said Obvious Adams, perched on the tiny rear seat, his knees around his ears. *"First impressions to the contrary, our Mr. Swift is quite a cautious fellow."*

"So, what's up?" asked Jeremy. "You find some silver bullet that'll fix everything?"

As he accelerated around an 18-wheel Peterbilt, I said, "This is something we don't want to rush."

"You've still got nothing?" It was more a statement than a question.

"On the contrary. I've given Swift SurBotics a lot of thought. There's plenty we can do, but focusing on today is too narrow. We need a strategy that looks down the road and takes us beyond bidding on business, over and over."

Jeremy found cruising room in the middle lane and up shifted. I went on pointing out that SSI needed to adjust the way it looked at customers and sales. Not a cure-all - a long-term immunization.

He turned on the traffic report, noted a slowdown on the westbound I-40 and tapped the GPS for an alternate route. "Yeah, I get the long-range stuff," he said, "but the shit's flying, right now. How's that factor in?"

"It means we start sooner."

I left Jeremy to concentrate on driving. As we pulled into the parking lot at Raleigh-Durham International, he asked, "What's this going to cost me?

"One-point-three million, plus my fee."

He took the keys from the ignition. "One-point-three. Let me guess: you want to give away an MX."

"Not exactly, but yes."

"Interesting. Write up a proposal. I'll look at it." He got out, slammed the door and began running toward a private plane, unimpeded by a briefcase or other luggage.

Obvious Adams said, "One might guess that with your own plane, you could set your own schedule. I wonder what's so urgent in Texas?"

It was a good question, but I had a more immediate one: stranded here in nowhere land, how could I find a taxi?

CLIMATE

All small, publicly traded R&D companies follow a similar business model: come up with a new product idea, sell the story to shareholders and financial backers, spend your development dollars wisely, wait for regulatory approval, sell enough to get beyond the breakeven point, then keep selling to maximize the return. Or sell the licensing rights to a third-party marketer, as early as possible, and move on to the next project. At every point it's about selling something - ideas, evidence, product - and it works well for those companies that survive. For Swift SurBotics, the model had stalled.

SITUATION

There was a chain of reasoning I didn't get a chance to explain to Jeremy. An MX-series robot sells for $1.3 million, a fairly big-ticket purchase. Developing the machine had cost some $60 million - cheap by health care standards, but still too high for a single sale to have much impact on the bottom line. The same could be said about the cost of giving one away. Breaking even would call for a couple dozen sales and might take many *months. With thousands of hospitals, the outlook seemed bright enough as Jeremy said; one or two major deals might be all it took to get things rolling. But at the rate SSI was moving - with a cash crunch and the clock ticking on investor patience - the near term was looking grim.*

VIEWPOINT

Of course, Jeremy knew all this. But again, what if we thought less about selling and more about helping? Swift SurBotics and its customers were keen to improve medical treatment. Everybody was interested in new surgical techniques - minimally invasive, remote controlled, maybe even unmanned - and while the hospitals had the clinical experience to validate new technology; nobody knew that technology better than SSI. The right relationship could concentrate these different strengths on a common pursuit - advancing the cause of minimally invasive surgery. It was the same strategy we had used at Meloche Communications - establish trust by helping clients in unexpected ways, develop a shared vision, and create a more collaborative, more productive, work environment.

51

TARGET

SSI needed to inject confidence into the market by announcing a high-profile deal. And the hospitals - Meisner, especially - could benefit from a reputation for leadership in minimally invasive surgery. When it came to raising awareness, what could capture the public imagination more than medical robotics? It brought science fiction into the realm of practical high-tech.

Those were the main points of the proposal I was drafting. Adams read it and said, "It looks like you're getting closer to the core, Bill. What action will you suggest?"

Here's what I saw. Swift SurBotics sits down with Meisner Medical and together they work out what I was calling an extended enterprise to advance the cause of minimally invasive surgery. Meisner contributes its know-how to help SSI modify the product, if necessary, and design features into the next series of robots. In return, Meisner gets the existing MX without charge until a new robot, built to its exact specs, is ready for market. A small share in future royalties will offset the costs of the one it commits to buy. The partnership has a five-year term, renewal subject to mutual agreement. And while it's an exclusive arrangement, SSI is free to form similar relationships with other medical centers interested in different areas like remote controlled or unmanned surgery.

Adams commented, "And I suppose you would be the obvious choice to broker the negotiations and publicize the alliance to the medical and investment communities."

The thought had occurred. I finished a formal proposal and e-mailed it to Jeremy Swift. Unveiling the strategy face-to-face would have felt more comfortable, but I was coming to accept the realities of a computer-dominated business environment.

"Have no fear," said Adams. "I suspect there will be plenty of opportunity for face-to-face discussion. You have written something with the potential to annoy a lot of people."

IT'S THE PEOPLE, STUPID

I nnovation is a hot buzzword because it's a driver of the global economy and necessary for business growth. Early adapters pay dearly to get it; average consumers want it at a reasonable price. Every company scrambles to deliver it, and there are shelves of books on the subject: how to stimulate innovation, reward it, profit from it, and keep it going by creating the right corporate culture. Many consulting practices offer comprehensive programs built around managing a portfolio of innovative practices that could include anything from new products to improved work processes to mergers aimed at acquiring innovation. I spent a lot of my time helping clients with new ways of looking at business relationships.

Promoting innovation has become an industry in itself - big enough that I suspect there's at least as much energy spent selling the concept as in coming up with something new. So here are a few popular myths.

Myth #1 – Innovation depends on individual genius.

There is a difference between creativity and innovation. Creativity is about coming up with ideas. Innovation is about implementing the best of those ideas; and today it's more likely to call on a whole team of techno-wizards rather than wait for a Thomas Edison to come along. Even Edison would tell you he didn't do it alone. There is also a difference between collaboration (people merely working together) and true integration, which is about galvanizing effort around a common pursuit. Advancing from collaboration to true integration has been the primary focus of the business relationships I have influenced over the years.

Myth #2 – Innovation is mostly about technology.

For American shoppers, there's nothing more compelling than new gadgets. As an example, the annual Las Vegas Consumer Electronics Show attracts over 3,000 exhibitors - 75 percent of the Fortune 100 companies - and more than 140 thousand visitors, all eager for a glimpse at the latest in audio broadcasting, cable, digital imaging, electronic games, home theater, and wireless. Sure it's exciting, but consider how many technologies have come to light at previous CES events - the VCR, Pong, laserdiscs, the Commodore 64 and Amiga computers, virtual reality games - and how many are now extinct or like music CDs, rumored to be on their way out, along with the companies that introduced them. A lot of new technologies have a surprisingly short run. The majority of new products - those that enjoy any measure of market acceptance - offer not so much a life-altering experience as a modest bit of feature creep, at best a few months advantage till competitors come up with something better. While innovation might be essential for growth, it's no guarantee of survival. And if it's about technology, it's also about something more lasting.

Hewlett Packard is one company that's launched its share of new technology but what sets it apart is seven decades of reinventing itself, through good years and bad, while moving the product lineup from audio testing and medical lab equipment to scientific calculators, personal computers, servers, software, hand-held data devices, printers, and with the acquisition of EDS, network integration, and information management. HP prides itself on a culture of innovation with a spotlight on not just technology but on collaboration across different areas within the company. Managers are encouraged to get input from outside their immediate work group and employees even hand out awards to those who provide additional help.

Myth #3 -- Innovation is more likely in smaller companies.

It's easy to imagine that fewer bodies and leaner management make for agile organizations geared to fast project approvals with minimal bureaucracy and politicking. Important as these advantages might be, they can be offset by some brutal realities. In the pharmaceutical industry, only 1 in 5,000 new drug ideas make it all the way from the lab, through clinical testing and FDA review, into the hands of prescribing doctors. Each winner costs in the neighborhood of $500 million to $1 billion in R&D, meaning that small drug developers are continually in danger of running out of cash before they get to market. Faster isn't always better; one misstep might bring a bright entrepreneurial company to its knees.

Larger companies, in contrast, can be hampered by a cautious decision-making process that kills off new ideas, but when they finally get around to a commitment, they have the organizational depth and financial cushion to weather setbacks. According to Harvard business professor Gary Pisano, it's a saw-off; the ability to introduce new products is split about equally between big and small pharma. The lesson: ideas are relatively easy to come by; the trick is bringing them to life. The other lesson: alliances between companies with vastly different strengths can make a lot of sense. And since like-minded people tend to produce a singular focus, collaborative teams often work better when they include a few mavericks.

Myth #4 – Innovation is complicated.

For this one, I'll draw on my experience in corporate communications. Admittedly, innovation can be extremely complex, but day-to-day most of us aren't working at the level of a NASA engineer. More often, it's the little things that make a difference.

One of the quieter innovations introduced by my former firm was a dress code for "techies" - common enough for employees, but a potential sore spot among those paid by outside suppliers. It's just that when attending formal events in New York or Toronto, I had long been struck by the odd note created when network video crews crawled through the crowd in jeans, stepping around women wearing designer gowns.

So whenever Meloche Communications staged high profile, black-tie events, we rented tuxedos for the production people, expecting plenty of objections. As things turned out, most of the crews enjoyed it; a few even mentioned how their normal dress had left them feeling out of place. A simple change of clothing made them part of the occasion, setting an atmosphere that added up to a more consistent evening for everyone, including the clients. Hardly the discovery of a new galaxy, but it made a positive difference.

Often I would invite this support crew to participate in onsite planning sessions with our own staff and all the other suppliers - audio visual specialists, writers, producers, theatrical directors, musical directors, actors, dancers, photographers, choreographers, set designers, and so on. This gathering was separate from the scheduled rehearsal, for which they were paid, but I wanted everybody to get the big picture and understand what we were trying to accomplish together. Many of the "techies" would invariably offer "non-technical" ideas that contributed to not only the event at hand, but future projects as well. For example, in one case, a supplier recommended that we invest in a permanent, high-quality set that could be easily modified for future use. The idea saved Meloche Communications over a million dollars a year, while significantly enhancing our productions. Evidently, we were the only house that invited "techies" to such meetings, and it taught us a lesson: people would rather be asked to help than bombarded with vague appeals to come up with good ideas.

In my mind, the exchanges we pioneered, capitalizing on the experience of our supplier network, foreshadowed today's thinking on supply chain management. Also, much like film or theatrical producers, we assembled a temporary group of diverse, talented, highly motivated people, only to disband them when it was time to move on. This has since become a standard business model in the biotech world. In some ways, the people who start and run these businesses are more like project managers than traditional CEOs,

Myth #5 – Innovation is mostly about technology.

This is such a wrong-headed idea that it's worth repeating. It brings to mind a story that covers much of what I've learned about innovation over the years, involving just about everything - except technology.

Travelers' checks in some form, go all the way back to the late 1700s, but their invention is usually credited to Marcellus Fleming Berry, an American Express employee who came up with the idea in 1892 after his boss J.C. Fargo returned from London, complaining about trouble getting money through a letter of credit. For almost a century, the company dominated this market. A trip without American Express Travelers Checks was unthinkable; the company's offices around the world became a home away from home where travelers stopped by to not only convert paper into cash, but also to pick up their mail.

Times change and by the 1980s with the growing popularity of credit cards, the company found itself sharing the global travel market with traditional banks. Customers would go into a bank asking for Amex checks and walk out with a competing product, which usually worked just as well and was cheaper. Clearly, change was in the wind, and as Amex's business shifted to card-based services, it started exploring new products to replace the once-dominant travelers' check business.

During that period, I was invited to a brainstorming session that included a group of American Express whiz kids, along with a high-level representative from their advertising agency Ogilvy and Mather and a senior management consultant from McKinsey. Because my firm orchestrated the lion's share of the company's global meetings, they thought I might have some insights about internal communications.

Up for discussion was a new idea: using the American Express Card to help corporate clients manage travel-

and-entertainment expenses. The concept was straightforward. Corporate clients would issue cards to their employees, and Amex would deliver a variety of services built around reports that helped businesses manage one of their biggest costs more effectively. The business travelers would get better service and Amex would realize a windfall in card charges and business-travel revenue.

It sounded like a classic win-win. To my surprise, the idea met a wall of resistance, especially from the financial people who glommed onto the liability risks. Many of the traditional marketing people were also against it. While they were used to reaching out to card members, this new product was strictly business-to-business and in their view, less sophisticated than research-driven consumer marketing. They were most comfortable backing up strategies with mountains of data; and they had little data on the corporate market. At that point, I offered my one and only comment, pointing out that my business was all about selling to corporations. If I had the American Express brand behind me, I'd be excited about knocking on corporate doors with a product that could save companies money. *What would they lose by developing the service as a trial, with cooperation from a potential client?* With that, I shut up. Eventually the meeting ended, my contribution having been absorbed in silence. I left with the thought that the Corporate Card was pretty much DOA.

About a year later, I got a call from Bob Greenfield, the recently appointed VP for a new Amex division called Travel Management Services. TMS had developed a product called the Corporate Card - *piloted through Burroughs Business Machines* - and they were taking it to market using information gathered from the Burroughs success. First, they wanted to launch the card internally to a group of U.S. sales, marketing, and senior management people, so he needed help with the communications support.

He never mentioned the brainstorming session, and may not even have been aware it had happened. To this day, I have no idea if the go-ahead was influenced by my comment. But I did end up managing the TMS annual meeting for the next six years, working closely with Bob Greenfield, who I would rate as the best pure sales executive I have encountered before or since. Today, a group that started with forty people is a global enterprise with thousands of staff. Whether you travel to Hong Kong, Paris or Sydney, Australia, you'll find Amex offices flourishing on the strength of the TMS Corporate Card, along with a follow-up product, the Business Card, aimed at smaller organizations.

During the inaugural TMS staff meeting, Bob Greenfield acknowledged the difficulties in putting together this new organization. He addressed his team with the words, "We have put a lot of ourselves into marketing and selling this product. We have all played a role in inventing it. Nobody should be able to take that mantle of leadership or those customers from us. Nobody."

The room exploded in applause. That moment provided a fundamental lesson on the nature of innovation. Sometimes new ideas fail because the market isn't ready or the product is flawed or the lawyers and accountants can't get their acts together or unforeseeable events conspire against success. Sometimes everything looks right and an idea still fails. Sometimes it succeeds almost too well. These days similar products are so commonplace that the idea has become just another commodity. But as in so many other financial and travel related services, it was American Express who led the way - starting with a young group pulling together to build a business from scratch. In their minds, they were no longer employees; they owned this business. Their passion and the resulting success had little to do with technology. It had everything to do with pride, stubbornness, imagination, an entrepreneurial spirit, and a willingness to look beyond their own world for inspiration. In my view, that's what innovation is all about. I had more notes for Obvious.

- Innovation is about bringing together people with different perspectives
- Innovation is uncomfortable
- Innovation is more than ideas – it's execution
- Innovation is about people

COLD SHOULDERS

T he next meeting at Swift SurBotics was more-or-less the opposite of the last one - a tedious, ego-crushing affair that had me thinking fondly about playing golf in sun-soaked southern California. As usual, Obvious Adams was right: I had written a proposal with the potential to tick off any number of people. And all of them were sitting in SSI's boardroom when Jeremy Swift brought me in.

Not that anybody was hostile or even unfriendly, as we exchanged introductions and business cards. The problem was the calm, slightly patronizing tone with which each member of the senior management team dissected the proposal for bringing in the Meisner Institute as a strategic partner. Almost to my disappointment, Jeremy's smart phone was nowhere to be heard. I would have welcomed an occasional interruption.

George Skura, legal counsel, kicked off the bloodletting. "What you've suggested Bill raises major problems with intellectual property. The MX robot - and all our products, truth to tell - embody dozens of patents. Opening our technology to customers involves serious questions about who would own the licensing rights for years to come. And who would share the liability if a surgical procedure went wrong? This is treacherous ground. I'd recommend against it."

"Keep your chin up," advised Adams. *"It's nothing less than you anticipated."*

Next came Shirley Lomenski, VP of engineering, who described the difficulties in retooling the assembly line and writing SOPs - standard operating procedures, she explained patiently - to accommodate every tweak a customer might ask for.

Marketing VP, Alfredo Donnino, perhaps trying to be helpful, suggested that SSI might not have to take it that far. "Once we've got the customer on the hook, we can let them make changes when it's easy, and come up with reasons to back off, if things get tough. My guys are pretty quick on their feet."

Jeremy shot back, "That's not how we work. If we're going to have an alliance, it's got to be meaningful."

The HR director, whose name I continue to forget, went on at length, spelling out problems with training and morale if the staff's expertise and creativity were given a back seat to ideas from outside.

And so it continued from one end of the table to the other: Regulatory Affairs, Biomechanical Design, Government Relations, Clinical Development, and a host of others, weighing in on the negatives, ending with the CFO Mike Gooderham. "Bill, you've had a difficult couple of hours and I don't want to add to them. However, I am concerned about the precedent this sets for future sales, and the message it might send to shareholders and the street. Under no circumstances do we want to reinforce the idea that the only way we can move an MX robot is to give it away. But the final decision is up to Jeremy. Our responsibility is to make sure he gets input from all sides."

After trading a few pleasantries and thanks, the meeting wrapped up and the team disappeared.

"How you doing?" asked Jeremy as we walked toward reception. "At least they agree."

Reading my face, he backtracked. "Okay, they don't like it. But these are busy people. Any one of them could have blown off the meeting. They took it seriously, and I doubt there's anything they couldn't solve, if they work together."

"This is one time you should accept the client's reading of a situation," added Adams.

"You'll just have to give them more to work with. Can you?"

"You haven't said what you think," I answered.

"Still on the fence. There's something I can't talk about yet. Maybe your strategy will help. Maybe it won't."

"In that case," I said, "I'll have to stop and think."

BUSINESS IMPROVISATION

B ack in my office, I had another session with
Obvious Adams.

"So Bill, we certainly heard why your ideas wouldn't work. What could you have done to get people thinking differently?"

It took a while, but eventually I flashed back to some film courses I'd taken at UCLA. Every theater piece has two key components: the story and the players. In thinking about it, my SSI proposal didn't clearly outline where this story was going.

And I didn't get the characters caught up in the moment. I remembered a book that promoted a great way of doing that. Years ago Viola Spolin had written *Improvisation for the Theater,* introducing an approach to acting that mimicked what jazz musicians do: first listen, then add. That's how they improvise on the spot. For actors it translates into a technique called "yes–anding," which I later introduced to corporate clients as a way of encouraging more useful business meetings. I called it

71

Business Improvisation.

Consider a typical conversation:

Mary in Marketing: Instead of bidding out every project, why don't we think about an alliance with one or two of our contractors?

Jack in Operations: That'll never work. We tried that a few years back with horrible results. You can't trust those bastards. Sooner or later they will nail us on pricing.

The result: end of story.

Spolin's technique showed how rapid innovation becomes more likely when people with different perspectives, listen, then add something new. There's only one important rule: every follow-up statement must begin with "yes–and." With this one change a conversation might go like this:

Mary in Marketing: Instead of bidding out every project, why don't we think about an alliance with one or two of our contractors?

Jack in Operations: "Yes and that might work this time if we do a more comprehensive analysis of potential suppliers.

Tom in Finance: "Yes and I'll share my research on how alliances fit with your experience.

The result: a success story in the making.

Adams commented, *"You could have used that technique with Swift SurBotics."*

"Yes and next time, I will. Right after a little more stopping and thinking."

IS TRUST REAL?

In February 2005, while testifying before a Senate Commerce Committee, Disney's CEO Michael Eisner, accused the computer industry of promoting piracy. Although he didn't mention Apple specifically, he did single out an Apple advertising campaign - inflaming a long-standing antagonism between Eisner and Steve Jobs. And the feelings spilled over into relations between Disney and Pixar Studios - which Jobs also headed - fuelled in part by Eisner's repeated denials that he had deliberately slammed a rival. So a year later, when Disney bought out Pixar, industry pundits were skeptical about the chances for a successful merger. Eisner's words were in the congressional record and at heart these companies just didn't trust each other.

— § —

Questions about trust are hardly confined to high-profile mergers. They're common in almost every business relationship, especially in a global economy where the lines between partners, suppliers, and customers can get fuzzy.

— § —

During the post-retirement phase of my career, I did some work for FMI Corporation, a firm highly respected in the construction industry for its management consulting and investment banking expertise.

As one of its services, FMI would help utilities form more productive relationships with contractors, cutting time, cost, and risk from the construction delivery process. Sometimes, these relationships were based on a strategy that could be seen as slightly radical in the tradition-bound utilities industry. Rather than putting every project up for a separate bid, FMI encouraged long-term, multi-million-dollar commitments to just one or two suppliers - not in every case, but where it made sense after thorough analysis. Secure contracts enabled suppliers to apply economies of scale to doing more work, more profitably. And that was the plan.

All too often, these relationships would start with the best of intentions and break down for lack of trust. Utility people tended to ride herd on the contractors as if they needed constant vigilance, while the contractors would see the utilities as painfully bureaucratic with only one mission: to beat them down on price. FMI would try to head off these conflicts by helping clients pick contractors with the right fit, but invariably moving forward demanded a behavioral change in both parties. Or at least a sign that such change was possible.

That need was illustrated most dramatically in the case of one FMI client, a major natural gas utility. Not unexpectedly, during the lead-up to a new alliance, a group of middle managers became intent on slowing things down after realizing the deal would create a new, unfamiliar working arrangement. So early on, the utility's operations chief called a meeting with all the players to express his commitment and get the alliance off on the right foot. He presented an overview of a new, fully integrated governance team comprised of managers from the contractors and his own company. And it was all warm and cozy, with one noticeable exception: the reporting hierarchy excluded all his utility managers who had been dragging their feet; they just weren't on the org chart.

This client-supplier alliance has since generated

unprecedented savings for the utility, while meeting all the contractors' expectations. One uncharacteristic move from one farsighted senior manager was all it took to establish trust, demonstrating that the utility was willing to remove barriers and put as much into making the deal work, as it did into making the deal itself.

— § —

When organizations start thinking about working together, trust can arise early as a kind of unspoken consideration. Obviously or instinctively, whichever you prefer, first impressions matter. Differences in values, ethics, and corporate governance can kill the relationship long before people start doing the work. Hard numbers and documented evidence must validate the alliance to start with. Does the deal make financial sense? Are the terms mutually favorable? Will the parties be stronger, more competitive or more productive? It's only later, perhaps months after the fact, that the emotional rubber hits the road - particularly if things aren't working well and sometimes, even if they are.

I've seen enough of these alliances to believe that setting the tone early is important. If you can establish trust at the start - say, by helping a colleague or giving something away - the chances of success go up.

THE SUCCESS STORY PARADIGM

It's easier for companies to trust each other when everybody knows where they're going. Most business initiatives, including alliances, start out with a strategic plan and I've seen many definitions. Of course, my favorite is a simple one, "the essential things that need to be done." But the process for identifying those things is often far from simple.

During my initial post-retirement career, I worked closely with a number of consulting firms, supporting their change management initiatives with internal communications. The clients often showed an impressive ability to drill down, extract relevant data, decipher it, and turn it into a strategic plan. But in the end, if I asked, "What is this organization all about?" every senior manager would give a different answer - usually made up on the spot, despite having just gone through the strategic planning process.

From a communications perspective, it made me wonder: if the executives who write these plans can't describe them consistently, how can they expect their people to understand what's happening and why or where they fit or what it will mean to customers, suppliers, and shareholders? Statements about mission, vision, and values are useful, but often vague, while the comprehensive strategic planning document can be far too detailed.

That's the problem. Strategic plans become thick books. They're rarely read by anyone other than the executives who draft them and a lot of people zero in on the parts that relate exclusively to themselves. There's no overriding picture of what's being accomplished or how everybody will do it together. Many executives just distribute the plan and hold middle managers responsible for reaching their own narrow objectives after which the thing gets shelved until the team launches another round of strategic planning.

Thinking about the shortcomings of traditional strategic planning took me back, eventually, to a few screenwriting courses. Before a film goes into production, somebody writes a 30 to 40-word conceptual outline, capturing events and fitting them together so everyone understands what's happening. It's different than a typical executive summary because it speaks to all stakeholders and not just the crew and actors, but the audience as well. And it can't be done until the story has been developed.

In the corporate world, I often wished I could re-assemble the planning teams and have them draft that kind of outline. It was the missing link in getting people to buy in. Many of my consulting colleagues resisted because in their eyes, the strategic plan itself was their 'deliverable.' Once it had been delivered, helping people understand it wasn't their job.

But I saw it as my job. So I developed something called the Success Story Paradigm to help management teams communicate a clear understanding of where they are, where they're going, and how they'll get there. In my mind, alliances should play out along the lines of a classic success story. Consider movies like Apollo 13, Saving Private Ryan or The Dirty Dozen. Each involves different character types, unfamiliar with each other, who come together for a common pursuit. As a team, they overcome obstacles and achieve extraordinary results beyond what any of them could do alone.

Such stories are structured around *the beginning* (Act One) that gets attention, introduces the main characters, establishes a common bond like trust and near the end, provides a transition point that sets the story in motion.

The middle (Act Two) advances the story through a series of plot points, involving obstacles and conflicts, surprises, disappointments, successes and drives the story forward through situations that require spontaneous innovation.

The conclusion, (Act Three) brings the characters together to face an overwhelming challenge that galvanizes collective effort and leads to a satisfying resolution.

Traditional strategic plans will always be important, but the Success Story Paradigm can offer a more easily grasped and possibly, more realistic roadmap. It makes room for unexpected events and mavericks - people ready to explore new ideas without going off strategy. It plots a course that anticipates problems without necessarily identifying them and it calls on the players to make choices beyond the usual preconceived actions. Once this storyline has been developed, it becomes fairly easy to write a conceptual outline that lets managers describe what their organizations are all about.

I decided to share my idea with Obvious.

Success Story Paradigm

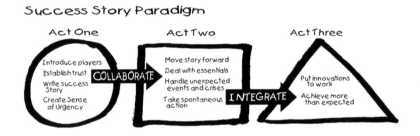

Adams commented, "It is more than simple, Bill. It is elegant. If a ninety-minute movie can portray the most complex events and relationships in a way that holds our attention, why should this same structure not work for business?"

As usual, he had grasped the obvious. And now, with a potential SSI-Meisner alliance on the horizon, we had a chance to put notions like the Help Ethic and the Success Story Paradigm to work.

82

WHAT'S MISSING?

T he next meeting at Swift SurBotics was preceded by the usual round of e-mails, telephone tag, and schedule juggling. At one point I wondered whether Jeremy had been right in thinking the senior management team really wanted to continue the discussion. The fog was cleared by one of his typically terse phone calls.

"Next Tuesday, Bill. 10 a.m. See you then." The connection clicked and he was gone.

— § —

So there we all were in the SSI boardroom: Jeremy Swift, George Skura, Shirley Lomenski, Alfredo Donnino, Mike Gooderham, the heads of Regulatory Affairs, Biomechanical Design, Government Relations and Clinical Development, and the HR director whose name I can never remember. They sat politely, staring at the presentation screen, taking occasional notes, as I went through the breakdown of my approach to collaboration using the Success Story Paradigm.

From the back of the room Obvious Adams raised his hand. *"Is this going well, Bill? Are they are getting the message?"*

I couldn't tell. Quiet comes in different flavors: absorbed, fascinated, bored, and comatose. This was just quiet. And I was doing most of the talking, which wasn't good.

Still, I kept talking, pointing out that while less systemized than Six Sigma, what I was proposing had a well-defined framework. I took them through Act I with the Help Ethic, bringing all the players together, establishing trust and creating a sense of urgency and in our case, the drive to create a whole new approach to surgery. Then came Act II: overcoming obstacles, anticipating that things might never go exactly as planned, and improvising as we went along. And finally Act III with an emphasis on the gains we could look forward to as a byproduct of rapid innovation.

There were no questions.

Instead, Jeremy said, "Good presentation. You've

given us a lot to think about."

Again, the usual thanks and handshakes, and the team was gone even Jeremy after asking his assistant to retrieve my visuals. His only other comment was to say we'd be talking soon.

Obvious Adams said, *"This isn't shaping up like a Success Story Paradigm."*

"Not yet," I admitted.

Something was missing or so I thought.

DEFINING A COMMON PURSUIT

S ome years ago, I sat in on a presentation by Daniel Vasella, CEO of Novartis, one of the world's largest pharmaceutical companies, as he took the audience through the highlights of developing a drug called STI-571, otherwise known as Gleevec.

In 1998, Novartis ran a small clinical trial with a handful of patients suffering from a rare form of leukemia, and much to the researchers' surprise, every case went into remission - 100 percent efficacy. Even so, there was a problem. Drug development is expensive and because the estimated number of patients was only 40 thousand worldwide, the market would be extraordinarily small. In other words, it would be almost impossible for the company to make money. So marketing had no interest in pursuing development.

And yet there was that result: 100-percent remission. How could anybody ignore that? Whether out of pride, stubbornness, instinct or ethics, senior management decided to ignore the numbers and not only move ahead with larger clinical trials, but to speed up the process. And when confronted by a shortage of drug, they persuaded staff to work in shifts, around the clock, simply by explaining what they were producing and why it mattered. Novartis finished the clinical trials in a record two years. Gleevec was then submitted to the FDA and approved within 10 weeks - another record at a time when regulatory review could easily take a year or more.

Dr. Vasella attributed the commitment to the fact that people not only saw the opportunity to make a difference, but clearly understood their own impact on the process. Today, Gleevec brings in $2.4 billion annually even though the company gives it away to some 15,000 patients who can't afford it. And there's a bonus, Novartis has since discovered the drug effectively fights other rare tumors and might also work against arterial disease and smallpox.

In many ways Dr. Vasella's story paralleled the innovation process outlined at Swift SurBotics. It also identified what I'd overlooked. In both scenarios, people with different skills were brought together. There were unforeseen obstacles to be overcome. And just as Novartis had set out to change the way leukemia was treated, we had an equally high-minded, far-reaching vision. But there was also a difference. While better surgical technology was a great long-term goal, we had no deadline and no common pursuit like the delivery of a breakthrough drug to motivate the SSI people. They were providing a free robot, period. Meisner would be pleased, but it wasn't enough. We needed a more compelling goal to get everybody moving.

And that's exactly what turned up in the form of another call from Jeremy late in the day.

"Bill, your proposal's a go. Check tomorrow morning's newswire. We're putting out a release."

A TRANSITION POINT

A t first, I didn't get Jeremy's meaning. It was far too early to announce anything about Meisner and we hadn't even met. But the news release not only explained why SSI's management team had been so distracted during my presentation, it supplied a sense of urgency to get Jeremy's team keenly focused on alliances.

SWIFT SURBOTICS BUYS DALLAS SCIENTIFIC FOR $1.2 BILLION

CHAPEL HILL, NC – Swift SurBotics Inc. (Nasdaq: SSIR), the world's leading developer of medical robots, today announced its intention to purchase 100-percent ownership in Dallas Scientific Group Inc., a privately held, family owned, medical devices company. Both companies have signed a letter of intent (LI). The purchase price has been set at $1.2 billion in cash and common shares of SSIR. The agreement is scheduled to be finalized on November 30 after the boards of directors for both companies have reviewed and approved the proposal.

"This merger extends our product line to a much wider range of models," said Jeremy Swift, chairman and CEO of Swift SurBotics.

"We also believe the expanded organization will improve our product development capabilities, making us the most competitive company in the industry."

Swift SurBotics (SSI) will pay Dallas Scientific an upfront amount of $15.9 million, plus annual installments of $2 million over the next 10 years, with the balance to be rendered in common shares, the exact amount to be calculated based on a weighted average of the share price during the five days immediately preceding the closing date.

In return, SSI will assume full ownership of all Dallas capital assets, inventories, receivables and liabilities, if any.

Both companies are committed to retaining the full complement of existing employees for the foreseeable future, and no changes in numbers, titles, or job descriptions are anticipated.

Edward Stone, president of Dallas Scientific said, "Our organization is excited to be working with Swift SurBotics. This relationship will provide the intellectual and financial support to continue R&D programs with our specialized line of small, portable robots."

At the same time, the news left me puzzled about my hopes for a long-term SSI-Meisner deal. It seemed to push the whole idea into the background.

"You might have mentioned something," I said to Jeremy over the phone.

"Couldn't. Selective disclosure rules."

"So what does it mean?"

"It means we're taking out the competition. Dallas has been kicking our asses with those little robots. And now we've got them in our pocket. And we're getting some clever engineering. For peanuts. Stone's retiring. Just wants out."

"Okay, but what does it mean for the alliance with Meisner?"

"More important than ever. Meisner provides solid clinical support and a big-name endorsement. We do the high end; Dallas concentrates on the portables; plus they've got a military contract to ruggedize models in hostile environments. *Most competitive company in the industry.* Hell, this alliance is gonna change the world. A win for all three of us."

So now we had to bring together three organizations - something I hadn't anticipated. The wheels began to turn. Do we work with everybody at once? Or start with two and add one later? Which two? I knew next to nothing about Dallas Scientific. How would its people react to the merger? Did they share SSI's commitment to stretch the technology?

Obvious Adams stepped in, *"Easy Bill. Remember the first advice you ever gave me: business is about stopping and taking time to think."*

Only we didn't have time. The Dallas merger was closing in six weeks and we needed to start talking to Meisner soon. Otherwise they might take the smaller robot and call it a day, leaving me and my alliance hanging.

"Take a few minutes anyway," insisted Adams.

With that encouragement I left the office early, drove home, walked Bailey, and took Ann out to dinner. And somehow, the answers came. Not all of them. Just one: I didn't have to tackle these questions by myself. I only needed to tap into the drive of the senior managers at Swift SurBotics. I began to feel confident. I was no longer trying to sell anybody on anything. I was simply trying to help. The senior managers had an immediate, concrete need to make the Dallas merger work. That was just the first step in changing surgical practice, as we know it. The rest we could map out together.

BUSINESS IS A THREE ACT PLAY

C ompared to our earlier get-togethers, the working sessions with SSI's management team were a transformation. The pace was brisk. The discussions, lively. The comments, candid and insightful. Jeremy Swift took on his natural role as leader, keeping the process on track, with me in the background as counselor and coach. Over the next two weeks, we came up with a Success Story Paradigm.

ACT ONE

- We begin by creating small staff groups from SSI and Dallas - no involved commitment, just enough to introduce people and let everybody in on the plan to attract Meisner.

- The focus shifts to the three-way alliance. Through a series of meetings, we roll out the vision of a leading research institute with Meisner at the helm.

ACT TWO

- Meisner gets new equipment, including a free MX-series robot, in return for providing the clinical information needed to refine the technology and set the stage for the next model.

- Meisner expands its educational program gaining new prominence as a teaching hospital. Dallas staff joins the team to help with training.

- The alliance continues to gain respect among medical professionals. Swift SurBotics uses its IT skills to develop a database that captures case study details as they come in and automatically updates documentation for peer-reviewed journals

- Meisner gains added recognition and royalties. George Skura, SSI's legal counsel, works with Meisner's advisors to negotiate contracts and resolve intellectual property issues. Defining the patent issues means all parties are free to share proprietary information.

- The entire alliance enjoys an open exchange of information and Meisner's fundraising becomes more successful. Alfredo Donnino and his marketing group collect ideas and bring in specialists from both organizations as needed.

- Dallas strengthens its product line while Meisner and SSI gain experience in new fields. All partners collaborate on the R&D needed to satisfy Dallas's military contract.

- The pool of expertise grows when needed. Other senior management - Regulatory Affairs, Biomechanical Design, Government Relations, Clinical Development and HR, along with their colleagues at Dallas - stand by to pitch in as necessary.

ACT THREE

- General awareness of the alliance remains high, along with interest in SSI's stock. I oversee the communications side, keeping the PR and Investor

Relations agencies updated, looking for opportunities to publicize the results of a successful collaboration.

- Within five years, the alliance of Meisner, SSI, and Dallas becomes *the* place to be, whether looking for training or new technology. Much of what will be discovered cannot be imagined today.

All this emerged from our first go-round at storytelling. If it seems to gloss over potential problems, it doesn't. It just acknowledges that we can't predict everything, and leaves room for the idea that whatever comes up - good or bad - will be handled as we move along.

As one of the immediate benefits, staff at SSI and Dallas Scientific were motivated to start working together from the start. I can't say they were completely comfortable about the merger, but the Meisner alliance did give them a common focus.

One regrettable consequence of all the activity was that, somehow, I lost touch with Obvious Adams.

Maybe, he thought I no longer needed him, or maybe

his disappearance was my fault. We'd made an appointment, which I missed because of a last-minute change to Jeremy's calendar. I even drove around looking for the Adams Roadhouse, but as in the beginning, it wasn't there. With no way to make contact, I kept hoping he'd just pop up. He didn't.

Inevitably, I continued spending more time with Jeremy Swift. With Obvious Adams, personal exchanges had been rare. I'd never learned much more than his name, Oliver, and the story about rising from a clerk in his father's grocery store to a career in advertising. By comparison, Jeremy's climb hadn't been nearly as steep, and he had no problem talking about himself. His parents ran a vineyard in the Napa Valley. He didn't drink alcohol. He owned a cabin in the Blue Ridge Mountains, but was hardly ever there. Mostly he was in his office or on the road - no surprise. He had started SSI on the same day he graduated from Duke. He had never married - again, no surprise - although there was a nephew with some kind of disability, and he funded a program for autistic kids. He also donated anonymously to several charities in the Triangle area. But still, like Adams, not an easy guy to know.

Act Three

Our protagonist learns that sometimes good

things don't have to end

SO WHERE IS OLIVER?

B y the time we were ready for the pitch, there hadn't been any sign of Adams for a month. I seemed to be flying solo, although with all the involvement from the SSI and Dallas teams, I was far from alone.

The first meeting at Meisner was a small affair - Dr. William Ahrens, the chief of surgery, Jeremy, and me. Rather than launching into the full-blown alliance scenario, we steered the conversation toward the upcoming merger with Dallas Scientific.

"We understand you were looking at the Dallas Apollo," said Jeremy, a reference to the specific model.

"Good machine," interrupted Ahrens. "We did a feasibility study."

"Just so you know; with the SSI-Dallas Scientific merger, whatever was on the table is still there."

"Nothing's on the table. The machine's fine. We just haven't decided."

It turned out; the problem was that the Apollo only had FDA approval for a limited range of procedures. In comparison, the MX didn't have any real shortcomings.

"The capabilities are enormous, but getting our residents up-to-speed will take much longer."

And that opened the door to how Meisner's experience might contribute to simplifying the interface - the benefits that could come from both organizations helping each other, no matter which machine the medical center picked.

With Jeremy in the lead, my thoughts wandered back to Obvious Adams. I missed him. What might he contribute to the discussion?

Jeremy said, "Bill, you look like something's on your mind."

"Only that we shouldn't forget SSI's marketing people. They have considerable communications savvy, which Meisner might find useful - say, in fundraising campaigns."

It was an idea I had floated with Adams and later, during the collaboration sessions with the SSI-Dallas team. Fundraising was a hot button with Jeremy. And as chief of surgery, Ahrens spent a lot of time trying to boost the center's profile and attract financial support. He suggested we all get together with Meisner's Carla Pratt, who as CEO, would have to weigh in on budget matters.

About a week later, while waiting for everybody's schedules to clear, a strange thing happened. Returning to my office, I ran into trouble opening the door. Something large and heavy was holding it back. Shoving as hard as I could, the door finally gave way enough for me to slide through. There, standing just inside, was a leather-upholstered, wingback chair.

Who would put a chair there? A joke? A present from Ann wanting to spruce up my workspace? She does like antiques and it certainly had some mileage. The only clue was a handwritten note stuck to the chair, "Use it wisely." That's all it said.

I called Ann. She knew nothing about it. I asked Laurie.

"There's a chair in your office?" Later, she admitted that two delivery guys had wheeled the chair in on a dolly. She'd signed the shipping receipt, but didn't remember the company, and there was no other paperwork.

All I can say is that even though the chair was quite handsome, it didn't fit the rest of the décor and was pretty uncomfortable. Most visitors avoided sitting in it. Still, having it in my office felt somehow *right,* and in those moments when I was struggling with an idea, it was surprising how often inspiration would show up while gazing at this odd piece of furniture.

OBSTACLES CAN BE HUMAN

T he next Meisner meeting included the same cast, with the addition of CEO Carla Pratt. Plus an unexpected development. Ms. Pratt began by pointing out that Meisner needed two robots, one for classroom teaching and another for the OR. Then she introduced what I saw as a major obstacle.

Surgeons, like star athletes, are not created equal. The most skilled are called "luminaries" since their reputations boost an institution's prestige and can affect the fundraising potential. And because of their position they can wield a lot of power when it comes to buying decisions. The Meisner Medical Center had two such luminaries.

Dr. Indira Mujrhadi, a neurosurgeon, wanted both robots to come from SSI. She was looking for consistent training and she liked how the MX handled. But there was an even bigger luminary, Dr. Zhivago (not his real name), a gifted cardiac surgeon with an ego the size of Montana. He had honed his robotic skills on the Dallas

Apollo and did not want to start over with a different machine. Carla Pratt controlled the Meisner's budget, but she would have trouble overruling Zhivago.

There were stories about hospital administrators who had invested in expensive equipment, only to have it gather dust because a luminary's followers ignored it.

As it was, Meisner could afford one machine; two would be a stretch.

"Besides not wasting money," said Pratt, "I'd like to keep a lid on the professional rivalry between these departments.

It was a good opening for Jeremy. "Interesting you should bring that up. Now that we're merging with Dallas Scientific, collaboration is something close to our heart. We see this as a big opportunity for Meisner."

He launched into the vision for a new kind of medical entity, an advanced surgery Mecca to include SSI and Dallas Scientific with Meisner at the hub leading the way in research, technology and scientific innovation.

"Last time you mentioned helping us with fundraising," Ahrens said with a glance at Pratt.

"For sure, that's something we can help with. Bill can take us through the preliminaries."

I provided an overview of The Help Ethic, Extended Enterprise Relationships, the Success Story Paradigm and the potential for building a fundraising campaign built around a new medical superpower.

Pratt commented. "I like the big picture. But Dr. Zhivago and he's a wonderful man, don't misunderstand, but Dr. Zhivago believes *he's* the big picture. He doesn't always play well with others."

"Let's go with that thought," I said. "Meisner's a great hospital and a great school. But if I was a name surgeon, I'd want a hand in building the world's leading medical robotics institute. Dr. Zhivago would be front and center."

Pratt and Ahrens smiled politely and exchanged knowing looks. Jeremy pressed on with the plans for a follow-up meeting. The idea was to bring together the key people from SSI and Dallas, along with the chiefs of all Meisner's surgical disciplines, the R&D group, a few leading professors, and the head of nursing. Ahrens suggested we run it as a workshop and volunteered his staff to work on the details. Jeremy suggested that, as a specialist in communications, I act as facilitator.

On our way to the parking lot I asked Jeremy, "Why me, moderating a session with all these science heavyweights? What do I know about surgical procedures or robotics?"

"Remember the first time we met? You didn't want to talk about technology? I got it. You wanted to talk about relationships, and Zhivago sounds like a relationship-and-a-half. If he gets stuck on an Apollo, Mujrhadi could feel left out and we're back to turf wars and there goes the alliance."

He stopped walking. "If they go with an Apollo, our board's not gonna be thrilled, either. This Dallas thing isn't a done deal. The board's worried about what happens to the share price if we announce an acquisition while revenue's down."

"One way or another, Meisner's set to buy a machine," I said. "Why not give them an Apollo and they can buy the MX? In fact, maybe we can work out a way they can afford two MXs. Everybody wins."

"Everybody wins, if the merger goes through. Otherwise, we're back to where we started. No matter what, Zhivago sounds like trouble. Your job is to make sure everyone gets on one side, especially him. Don't be afraid to pull out all the stops."

A MEETING OF THE MINDS

I found myself thinking about the significance of business meetings. How many times had crucial decisions come down to the success or failure of a single event? Here was another one. In my mind, there was only one reason for having a meeting: to generate a change in the participants. If people left knowing or thinking the same things as when they started, we were wasting everybody's time. With Meisner we wanted everyone to buy into a new, larger relationship, but as Jeremy had suggested, by *everyone*, we really meant Zhivago. He could torpedo this deal. So what would cause him, and everyone else to move in the direction we wanted? How do you make someone want to be part of an extended enterprise when he's used to being the center of his own universe?

Back in my office, there was still no word from Obvious Adams. I sat staring at the leather wingback, hoping for inspiration. As if the chair's very presence wasn't strange enough, I swear some days it would move. Not across the room or anything, and not while I was watching, but now and then I'd look up and find it a few inches to the left or right from where I'd remembered it. It was like something out of Steven King. Or a weird theatrical prop.

Prop, stage play, theatre -Business Improvisation.

That's what we could try with Zhivago. Get him and the whole group "yes–anding." If it seemed a little contrived, what the heck. Jeremy had said not to hold back. And that's when I got another idea, which in comparison, was over-the-top.

THE ROUND TABLE

Among mail services, Canada Post stands out for covering the largest geographical area on the planet. It maintains almost 7,000 outlets, with 6,000 vehicle routes, 15,000 carriers and 72,000 employees in total. Every day, it delivers 40 million pieces to 14 million households spread across an area slightly larger than the continental United States. I know this because Canada Post used to be a Meloche Communications client, and at the outset of our relationship, the CEO Don Lander took me into his operations center and explained it.

Lander was a former CEO of Chrysler Canada under Lee Iacocca and had been brought into Canada Post to streamline operations. The room we were standing in was his creation - banks of computers, and walls of monitors displaying every postal station, vehicle and route, along with weather conditions, road construction, airline routes, and ground traffic. The enormity of highlighted maps, scrolling data and flashing lights was not so much a celebration of technology as a visual assault, and I was impressed. When I said so, Lander waved it off.

"Know the most important piece of technology in here?" he asked. "It's right there." He pointed to a large round table in the middle of the room. This was the operations table where key managers would gather every day for an update.

"Know why it's round?" he asked again. "Because it makes people look at each other. Not so easy to ignore the guy down at the end or blame him not when he's sitting right across from you, eye-to-eye."

A round table. Simple. Low-tech. Yet as a communications tool, highly effective. Not only did people look at each other, they tended to listen. And add. Just as in improvisation.

It was a perfect stimulus for our three-way workshop. Everyone would be in this thing together without dominance from one end of the table like most boardrooms. Of course, a round table would also set the stage; the over-the-top part was what would come with it.

If that mysterious chair could move around my office, maybe it could move into our workshop.

EXPECT THE UNEXPECTED

I 've mentioned the need to make room for unplanned events. Sometimes, you just get lucky. Turning to the business section of the Raleigh *News & Observer*, one item jumped out.

HIGH-TECH SWIFT SURBOTICS CONTINUES TO GROW

Chapel Hill, NC – Robotics leader Swift SurBotics Inc. and Texas-based Dallas Scientific Group Inc. have announced they're joining forces.

Under an agreement signed today, Dallas Scientific becomes a wholly owned subsidiary of SSI. The takeover deal, estimated to be worth over $1.2 billion, creates the country's largest developer of surgical robots, controlling a 95-percent share of the market.

"Most immediately, this merger strengthens our product line, providing a broader range of models," said Jeremy Swift, chairman and CEO of Swift SurBotics. "We're looking forward to some exciting progress in delivering better tools that benefit health care professionals and patients."

In early trading, SSI's share price declined by $2.15, (13.7 percent below the day's opening).

"Congratulations," I said to Jeremy over the phone later that day. "You did it."

"Uh, yeah. You see the share price? I expected a drop. But thirteen freakin' percent?"

"Surely it will bounce back," I offered.

"It better, and fast. Had to make a deal with the board. If the price isn't up within two months, I'm gone. This workshop better work."

The next day, I received an invitation:

PLEASE JOIN US

PROGRESS IN MINIMALLY INVASIVE SURGERY

A HALF-DAY WORKSHOP SPONSORED JOINTLY BY
MEISNER MEDICAL CENTER, SWIFT SURBOTICS INC.
& DALLAS SCIENTIFIC GROUP
FOUR SEASONS HOTEL

———◆———

PRESENTERS:
JEREMY SWIFT, PHD, MBA, PRESIDENT & CEO
SWIFT SURBOTICS

WILLIAM AHRENS, MD, CHIEF OF SURGERY
MEISNER MEDICAL CENTER

FACILITATOR
WILLIAM J. MELOCHE

———◆———

RSVP

Carla Pratt

CARLA PRATT, CEO
MEISNER MEDICAL CENTER

THE EXTENDED ENTERPRISE

J ust because I couldn't locate Adams, doesn't mean he couldn't be part of this, and in the days leading up to the Meisner workshop, I got my assistant Laurie working with Dr. Ahrens's staff to do some stage managing.

"A round table?" Laurie asked.

"Right"

"And you want to seat twenty-five?"

"Right"

"And you want place cards for everybody, including this Oliver Adams, who's not on the list."

"Yes, please."

"That's a big table. You doing this in Camelot?"

Despite the sarcasm, the work got done. After a lengthy search, Dr. Ahrens's staff found the right table and had it shipped to the hotel, although they had to relocate to a larger function room. Meanwhile, I primed a few key participants, mostly Carla Pratt, Dr Ahrens and a late addition, Dr. Kim Jung from Dallas Scientific.

On the day of the workshop, the crowd gathered - SSI and Dallas staff members, the chiefs of four Meisner surgical departments, the head of R&D department, a few professors and the head of nursing, plus Dr. Mujrhadi, Dr. Ahrens, Carla Pratt, and Jeremy. A tent card reading Oliver Adams sat on the table in front of an empty chair, the very same leather wingback that had appeared so mysteriously in my office.

Everybody chatted while Pratt, acting as host, checked her watch. About fifteen minutes after the scheduled start, a tall, handsome fellow, wearing rubber clogs, surgical scrubs and a funny flowered cap swept in with a flock of interns and residents in tow. This had to be Dr. Zhivago.

"Hey Carla, everybody, sorry to keep you waiting." Zhivago eyed the leather wingback, and then took the only other remaining seat at the table while his entourage found stacking chairs against the wall.

Carla Pratt made formal introductions, summarized the different backgrounds represented in the room, and introduced me.

I began with a prediction that within a decade people would remember the day the Meisner-25 gathered to make medical history. By that time, surgical procedures in many different fields will have been converted from open to closed. And the achievement will be credited to the health care professionals, scientists, technologists, entrepreneurs, and teachers who came together on this day, ready to share their knowledge.

"This will happen," I promised, "because we are all starting this workshop with a single mindset: to help each other help patients." And with those words I turned over the floor to Dr. Ahrens.

Ahrens, following a suggestion I'd passed along, opened with a success story that described the impact of surgical robotics on the different disciplines represented at the table, describing future events as if they had already happened. It prompted Dr. Mujrhadi to talk about the neurosurgical discoveries that would be needed to make this vision workable. "But that is my perspective," she said. "Perhaps I should ask some of you to share your experience and challenges."

Each of the surgical heads expanded on the role minimally invasive surgery might play in improving treatment for patients in pediatrics, obstetrics, urology, and trauma medicine.

Dr. Kim Jung, Dallas Scientific's head of bioengineering, reviewed a history of computers and their impact in areas such as aerospace, reinforcing the message that "closing" all surgical procedures was by today's wisdom, a scientific impossibility. Just as today's technology had been equally impossible only a decade ago.

Jeremy followed with a description of past and present robotics advances, pointing out that whatever we had now was bound to fade away, and that organizations like Meisner, SSI, and Dallas Scientific could work together to create the breakthroughs that would advance the world of minimally invasive surgery. The talent to do that was right here in this room.

This was my cue to talk about the prospects for a

useful alliance between business and health care professionals, based the help ethic.

"Before going on," I said, pointing to the empty chair, "let me introduce our missing guest."

I talked about Obvious Adams, skipping our more recent mentoring partnership, (as well as a possible invitation to Meisner's psychiatric department), and retold the *Saturday Evening Post* story about a fictional icon who after doing his homework came up with stunningly obvious answers that somehow hit the mark.

"I want to believe," I said, "that Obvious or Oliver to use his given name, still has a place and is in fact with us as represented by that chair, a testament to radical, outrageous ideas brought to life in a straightforward, common sense way. He's the guiding spirit behind this extended enterprise. Like all oracles, we can't necessarily see him. But he's there.

Dr. Zhivago started to laugh. "This is silly."

"Yes, it is silly," I said, "and it's useful. Because of him, we're actually sitting here, talking about helping each other do impossible things to help patients. He's the inspiration behind this alliance. Moving forward will require collective imagination."

It was time to inject some Business Improvisation. I reviewed the "yes–anding" rules, but before we could start, Zhivago laughed, "Yes–and I know this game."

As I said, sometimes you just get lucky. By pure co-incidence, Zhivago had a daughter in theater school. She had introduced the exercise years ago as a way of handling family disputes.

"Yes," I said, "And we can start moving this alliance forward."

Jeremy added, "And SSI and Dallas can get the practical insight to continue moving minimally invasive surgery forward."

Ahrens joined in, "And Meisner can get some much-needed funding."

Zhivago said, "Yes and we can we get the equipment we need, right now."

And Carla Pratt capped things off. "And all you doctors will help us set the standard for MIS excellence worldwide."

Zhivago laughed again. "Ladies and gentlemen, there are bigger issues here than which robot we should train on. I believe we've got a job ahead of us in the best interests of our patients, so let's get on with it."

So maybe the discussion didn't go exactly like that. But it's how I remember it. And whether or not Zhivago really bought into the extended enterprise, the thought of playing a lead role in an even more prestigious center had its appeal. A big fish in an even bigger pond. So he threw his support behind the relationship, particularly after Ahrens outlined the details of how Meisner would get the immediate use of an Apollo, plus a deal that included two MX-series robots, data collection and research support, fundraising help, and the ability to influence the technology of minimally invasive surgery for years to come.

As simple as that a success story began to emerge that was initiated by Swift SurBotics; that would create a competitive advantage for the Meisner Institute and that would make life better for surgical patients around the world.

This workshop became a turning point. Within a week, the alliance partners had hammered out a firm agreement among Meisner, SSI, and Dallas. The robots were delivered and different groups in all three organizations began working together, drafting success stories around training, communications and collaborative R&D projects.

The alliance continued on a reasonably smooth course, with an occasional speed bump to keep things interesting. Many of the collaborative techniques introduced during the SSI-Dallas merger were carried over to the Meisner team sessions. From what I hear, some groups even used round tables at their initial meetings, although the wingback chair somehow found its way back to Raleigh.

Jeremy and I would occasionally dine out on the theatrics at that first workshop.

"Nuttiest business stunt I've seen," he would say. "We went in there as engineers, serious scientists, health care professionals. And we gave them the Twilight Zone. Lucky they didn't call security. Pays to take a risk sometimes."

I reminded him, "Was it farther out than buying a competitor when your cash was down? And sales, too?"

Jeremy grinned. His smart phone went off and he flipped it open. "Yeah, I'm listening."

And as he listened, he looked over at me and mumbled, "Looks like this relationship focus is paying off."

By paying off, Jeremy meant sales of the MX-series were on the rise. Within six months of announcing the Meisner alliance, a dozen hospitals bought the machines and seven more bought Apollos. One of Meisner's surgeons returned from reserve duty overseas and got heavily involved in the Dallas Scientific military project, leading to an extension of the contract. And SSI's share price doubled, partly because of sales and partly thanks to stories appearing in *BusinessWeek*, the *New York Times* and *Fortune*, al highlighting the company's new position at the forefront of health care R&D. Jeremy even got a spot on Larry King. His smart phone went off during the interview.

Meisner's latest fundraising drive set a new record of $21 million - easily covering the cost of the robots - much to the delight of Dr Ahrens and Carla Pratt. Thanks to new data analysis software from SSI, Dr. Indira Mujrhadi quickly published two papers in the *New England Journal of Medicine* and picked up three NIH grants after which Dr. Zhivago switched to the MX and began demanding changes in SSI's latest series, still under development. He also lobbied for the Meisner-SSI-Dallas alliance to adapt a distinct name and a committee was formed to make a decision. Personally, I think a new organizational identity is a great idea, but I'd like to suggest Oliver Adams as a namesake. To me, the Zhivago Institute sounds farfetched.

EPILOGUE

T he leather wingback chair is now in my office, once again. Although it doesn't appear to move around as much as it used to, strange things continue to happen. And none stranger than the other day. I happened to look over and noticed a piece of notepaper on the seat. I didn't recall leaving it there. Here's what it said:

Dear Bill,

Apologies if you felt abandoned. However, we both know that the final leg of your parable was something best completed on your own. I would like to express my appreciation for the experience and leave you with some lessons learned from our many encounters.

There is no cookbook for success. Obvious answers do not come easily. However, they can be found by taking a few, reasonably simple steps:

1) Stop, think and adopt the Help Ethic.

2) Decide who is helping whom and put yourself in the loop.

3) Imagine an integrated success story and write it down.

4) Expect the unexpected and when surprises come up, use them.

5) Earn trust through an early discretionary action.

I understand that as a result of your recent experiences you have become a sought-after speaker at business events. Congratulations and best of luck in this new endeavor. Perhaps we will meet again.

OA

WHAT CAN WE LEARN FROM THIS STORY?

A groundbreaking relationship usually starts with a big strategic idea that links your company, your B2B customer and the end user around a common pursuit that is bigger than products or services.

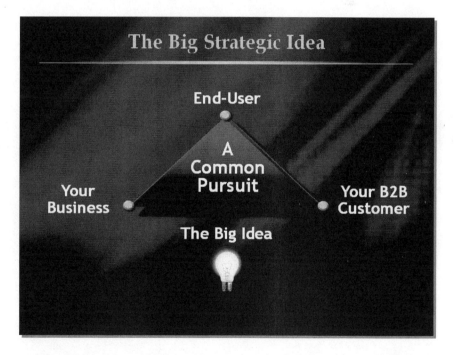

Coming up with that idea is the most crucial and challenging part of this process.

PILLARS OF PERFORMANCE

T here are four simple, yet challenging elements that I call "pillars of performance" that need to be aligned with the guidelines that Obvious Adams left me in his note: *The Help Ethic; The Success Story Paradigm; Business Improvisation and The Extended Enterprise.*

TARGETING THE RIGHT B2B
RELATIONSHIP

A "groundbreaking relationship" is defined from the supplier's perspective as **"<u>a business deal with a new or existing account that outperforms current B2B relationships by a factor of ten.</u>"**

The times-ten potential refers to key measures of performance including incremental top-line revenue potential or potential contributions to gross profit, net profit or productivity improvements. If it meets those criteria, it can become the sort of transitional deal that will put any company on more solid ground, thereby setting the tone for unprecedented growth.

This is why Obvious Adams suggested that we start by doing something that is rare today - *"stop and think."* There are two things we need to stop and think about. First, we needed to determine that *the times-ten potential* was there.

Second, we had to create that all important *"big strategic idea."* In this case, I worked exclusively with the CEO (sometimes I work with a designated relationship innovation team as well) on coming up with that idea - which is always expressed as a greater good on behalf of an end-user. The task requires that we put another rarely used tool to work - our collective imagination. The idea had to be strategically relevant to this targeted account - something they would not be able to accomplish on their own. The Meisner Institute had a unique collection of luminary surgeons across all minimally invasive disciplines. Swift Surbotics offered unmatched intellectual capital in the field of medical robotics. So a common pursuit or (greater good) was born:

"...establish the Meisner Medical Center as the global center of excellence for robotically-assisted minimally invasive surgery."

With this big idea in hand we were in a position to align our four pillars of relationship performance with the guidelines so wisely offered by Obvious Adams.

FIRST PILLAR - ADOPT THE HELP ETHIC

O bvious Adam's suggestion for *"Adopting the Help Ethic"* seems like a basic approach, but is very hard to do for sales-driven entrepreneurs. We have to meet with the CEO of that B2B customer, table our big idea, and possibly not even mention our product or our service. We simply need to know that a requirement for our stuff will be a byproduct of forging a groundbreaking relationship. We need to develop a mindset that shifts from "selling" to "helping." It may be natural to be obsessed with our technology, but in this case, we need to become obsessed with the strategic direction of the targeted CEO and how we can help him/her get where he/she wants to go. That means having a handle on the strategic priorities of their executive team. There are many ways to do that including conducting advance informal interviews with their key people, talking to some of their customers and researching their mission, vision, values and (if they have one) their strategic statement reflecting their game plan.

We had to do that homework before going in with our

big idea. Jeremy Swift and I were able to present the idea in the context of helping Meisner achieve a strategic goal that we knew would appeal to them. It may sound trite, but any B2B customer has to sense that we are not calling on them to sell our product or service; we have to actually develop a genuine desire to help. A good way to communicate that help ethic is to demonstrate some common ground by reflecting similar strategic priorities. People will believe that you have their best interests in mind when they sense that you have grasp of where they want to go and share their enthusiasm for getting there.

SECOND PILLAR - THE SUCCESS STORY

Obvious Adams' next step:

"Decide who is helping whom and put yourself in the loop."

This is where the Help Ethic becomes expanded beyond the relationship between your business and your B2B customer to include an end-user…usually your customer's customer. You can be assured that the strategic direction of your targeted account will involve providing that end-user with differentiated service. So "putting yourself in the loop" translates into how you can help your B2B account help its customers. Helping that end-user can often be seen as "that greater good" that extends beyond the basic product or service of either you or your B2B customer.

In this case, the end users were patients requiring surgery who could benefit from "closed" versus "open" procedures. Now we could take "our common pursuit" to another level. Patients (the end-users) would experience less trauma, quicker recovery times and reduced hospital time. Doctors from around the world have a place to go for the training and education needed to make all that happen. These aspirations were bigger than anyone's product. The achievement of such goals would comprise a true success story in which everybody would win - the patients, the doctors, the institution and my client. Telling that success story in advance would be the most compelling way to get the attention of the CEO, and at the very least, he or she would have to consider the merits of bringing this big idea to life.

Obvious Adams' next recommendation:

"Imagine an integrated success story and write it down"

I have developed a framework I call **The Success Story Paradigm** for telling B2B success stories. It uses the three act structure of a professional screenwriter or playwright.

The end results of the storyline do not have to be life-and-death benefits like those associated with open heart surgery. For example, a cleaning and maintenance company could decide to go to a major shopping center developer with the big idea - a collaborative process for keeping their malls as squeaky clean as Disney World. This would benefit shoppers who would have a more enjoyable shopping experience, the retail tenants who would get more business, the developer who would add a unique positioning point for leasing their space, and lastly the maintenance company could wind up with a global contract for cleaning all of their facilities rather than a few. Bringing that story to life in a compelling way is a talent that most business people do not have, yet it could be the crucial difference in making their biggest deal ever.

A compelling success story that tells of events before they happen will usually not close the deal, but it will set the stage by getting that CEO to agree that your big idea is worth considering. He or she should agree to have key people from both organizations evaluate its validity and come back with a recommendation to proceed or not. I recommend that you encourage the CEO to float the big idea internally and ask for volunteers rather than mandate it to people. Volunteers who explore a compelling success story are much more likely to come back with a supportive business case.

THIRD PILLAR - BUSINESS IMPROVISATION

In this parable, we convinced people to bring our success story to life by introducing principles of theatrical improvisation. Obvious Adams' recommendation:

"Expect the unexpected and when surprises come up, use them" - he was really calling for a more improvisational or agile way of moving things along more rapidly.

Today, we need to make things happen faster than normal. We had reached a point in this B2B relationship where people from both organizations needed to play off of each other's ideas and fill in the plot points of this emerging success story. The situation calls for more rapid innovation than occurs at traditional business meetings or within most strategic alliances. In this book, there is a crucial meeting among all the key players who have to come together to make this deal work. I introduced "business improvisational" techniques to create a working environment that was conducive to advancing the story in the moment and it worked. It boiled down to telling the success story in advance and encouraging people to listen and add their contribution to realizing the vision. That is precisely what I try to do in those vital meetings that follow a targeted CEO's decision to consider my client's big idea. The likelihood of them coming back with a recommendation to go ahead with this deal is increased substantially if positive momentum can be galvanized through a collective work environment.

In almost every instance, we end up with a business case being made to the targeted CEO from his own people. They will recommend going ahead with the deal, but there is still one more step to assure that the deal will work. We need to transition our B2B relationship from a group merely working together into a truly integrated effort focused on that common pursuit.

FOURTH PILLAR – THE EXTENDED ENTERPRISE

There is a difference between collaboration (merely working together) and true integration within what I call an Extended Enterprise Relationship. I define it as a working relationship between a supplier and a B2B customer in which they see each other as extensions of each other's enterprise. This brings us to Obvious Adams' final recommendation:

William J. Meloche

"Earn trust through an early discretionary action."

In the words of Stephen Covey, *"trust is the one thing that changes everything."* So how does that happen? The answer can come from asking ourselves a basic question. Why do we trust someone in any kind of relationship? The answer: *when they earn it* - most often because they do things for us without necessarily expecting something in return - the most fundamental aspect of the help ethic. I am not about to suggest that we start providing our products or services without charge, but there are times when the implications of a deal may be so big that to give something of value away in the early stages can be worth the effort. It can set the tone for trust, so neither party has to spend an inordinate amount of time trying to keep each other honest. The establishment of trust is what can move an extended enterprise relationship into high gear.

Mutual trust will streamline the process for not only making a deal, but also for making it work. In our parable I suggested to Jeremy Swift that he consider giving away a $1.3 million surgical robot. This was living proof that the ongoing relationship would be based more on helping than on selling. In fact, in the words of Obvious Adams, "selling is helping."

STRATEGIC INTERNAL COMMUNICATIONS

I built a global multi-million dollar business on the strength of a single idea: encouraging my clients to apply the same standard to strategic internal communications that was routinely used to communicate with external audiences. That's why I like to stick around for a bit after the deal is made and help get the success story communicated through this "extended enterprise." Key people from both organizations need to understand the success story, stay on track, and continue to play off each other's ideas. Most importantly, they need to take the kind of discretionary action that will make the deal work over a long haul.

The parable you have just read is based on a true story. I moved the whole scenario from California to the Research Triangle of North Carolina primarily, to not offend the sensibilities of the egos portrayed among some medical practitioners.

The stock of my client/supplier has increased by more

than a factor of ten and so has their top and bottom line performance. Today, the institution is recognized as a global leader in the field of medical robotics. Patients around the world are benefitting from less traumatic minimally invasive surgical procedures. The transition point in their success story began when this deal was made and has continued, in no small part because of effective internal communications within the extended enterprise.

IMPLEMENTING RELATIONSHIP INNOVATION

The one sure thing that is required to make these deals work - people in both organizations need to embrace the required change. I have developed a strategic internal communications process for expediting that process in the New Normal.

It begins with a customized success story told to everyone entitled *From Here to There*.

It continues by helping managers engage their people through guidelines entitled *Motivating Change*.

144

It culminates with guidelines entitled *Thriving on Change* - directed more at the people who must actually do the work.

I refer to my consulting specialty as **Relationship Innovation**. As far as I know I am the only one doing it. I suggest to my clients that they should continue to do their transactional selling well; but in today's world, it is a smart idea to be developing at least one groundbreaking B2B relationship on a CEO-to-CEO level.

From experience, I have found that the process for creating and closing a groundbreaking B2B relationship can be expedited in a 3-month period or one quarter. Overall, it boils down to the following 10 step-process:

Ten Steps to Relationship Innovation

Today	1.	Select a Strategic Innovation Team
	2.	Entrench the Help Ethic
	3.	Target a B2B Relationship
	4.	Create a Success Story Around a Big Idea
Set Date	5.	Present a Success Story Paradigm
Month 1	6.	Recruit Extended Enterprise Volunteers for the evaluation process
	7.	Engage Volunteers in Business Improvisation
Month 2	8.	Validate Success Story with a Business Case
Month 3	9.	Re-present Success Story as a Business Case
	10.	Begin Communicating for Change

Every day, I see more and more evidence that in the New Normal this may be the only way to stay ahead of the game.